KEVIN L SCOTT

THE 32K FORMAT

The CoParent's Transformation Guide To Becoming A Better Person And A Better Parent

A special thank you to my wife, Maria for believing in me and continuing to push and encourage me throughout the completion of this book. Those words of encouragement were the fuel that I needed to keep me going during this project.

Copyright © 2021 Kevin L Scott
All Rights Reserved.
No portion of this book may be reproduced in any form without permission from the author or publisher, except as permitted by U.S. copyright law.
ISBN: 978-0-578-84493-0

CONTENTS

About The Author
Important Note to the Reader
How to Use this Guide
Introduction
The Foundation of The 32K Format

The "3" C's
CONFLICT
Module 1K: Your Child Always Comes First
Module 2K: Let The Past Be The Past
Module 3K: Don't Let Conflict Scare You
Module 4K: Clarify, Don't Assume
Module 5K: Give Yourself A Chance To Think
Module 6K: Winning Isn't Everything
Module 7K: This Is A Business
Module 8K: A Time And A Place For Apologies
Module 9K: Seek Solutions, Not Retaliation
Module 10K: Be Open To Other Possibilities
Module 11K: Coparent, Don't Counter-parent
Module 12K: Relieve Stress and Take Your Time

COMMUNICATION
Module 13K: Avoid Communication Blocks
Module 14K: Language
Module 15K: Delivery
Module 16K: Listening
Module 17K: Consistency

COMMITMENT
Module 18K: Control What You Can Control
Module 19K: Agree and Stick To A Schedule
Module 20K: Be Flexible
Module 21K: Stay Focused
Module 22K: Seek Solutions

The "2" H's
HARMONY
Module 23K: From Resistance To Acceptance
Module 24K: Have Compassion

HEALING
Module 25K: Unresolved Anger Towards the Other Parent
Module 26K: Social Media Venting
Module 27K: Boundary Problems

The K
KNOW YOU
Module 28K: Don't Lose Yourself
Module 29K: Don't Lose Your Confidence
Module 30K: Be Aware of Your Trigger Points
Module 31K: Your Personality Is The Key
Module 32K: Self-Care

THANK YOU

ABOUT THE AUTHOR

My name is Kevin Scott, and I am the Founder and CEO of Build Your Wings Consulting, LLC. I have a passion for adding value to coparents by helping them transform into better communicators for themselves and their children. I believe in order for coparents to have true success, they must be willing to first, invest in their own personal growth and development. This is why I make it my mission to ensure that I positively influence coparents and challenge their perspectives to not look behind them at the things they cannot change but to look forward towards better relationships.

For over 20 years of my life, I have been a coparent and what I have learned from my life experiences as well as my research, studies and the conversations I've had with other coparents is that there was a need for a program that could help them resolve conflicts related to their coparenting relationships. One common thing that I have learned is that the communication issues between the two parents can make it hard on parents and the problem becomes evident when both parents can't seem to come to an agreement, and nothing can be resolved. And that is why I wanted to use my life experiences and training to help coparents work to improve themselves.

AN IMPORTANT NOTE TO THE READER

This book provides information about helping coparents transform into better version of themselves. The information is intended to help you become aware of how to manage and be more successful in your role as a coparent.

You will receive various ways in which you can improve if it applies to your specific situation. Therefore, before you proceed, I ask that you make a commitment (for yourself and your children) to use this information with the understanding that the other parent may not have the same level of commitment as you.

Every coparenting relationship is unique, and the advice and information provided addresses general techniques and behaviors that you may benefit from. Just know that these techniques are not suitable for situations where the health and safety of you or your children are put into question. In those situations, seek the proper authorities, legal assistance or a therapist, if needed.

HOW TO USE THIS GUIDE

This guide is designed to help you identify areas of your life where there may be room for improvement – one module at a time. It is meant to give the reader assistance when dealing with situations and emotions that pertain to coparenting. Also, this guide is not all encompassing and so it is not intended to answer all the scenarios that you and your coparent may encounter; however, it will give you some insight into what you can do to learn from and better your situation.

INTRODUCTION

I remember it like it was yesterday. It was November 8, 2012 and I was sitting on another telephonic court case between myself and my ex-wife. This particular case was regarding whether or not I owed her any back-child support. All was going well, and the judge said, "I'm setting up ongoing child support at $800 plus $50 arrears per month until the youngest child turns 18."

I thought to myself, that will be okay, no problem.

And that's when it happened.

The judge said, "What's the total arrears?"

Now I don't know who it was but all I could hear was "click...click...tap...tap...tap...click...click...tap...click...tap...click...click" and then there was a mumble.

Then the judge said, "Thirty-two thousand, one hundred and six dollars!"

My stomach dropped, I got light-headed and my mouth began to water. I then asked, "I'm sorry, I could barely hear you. What was that again?"

The judge didn't even answer my question, the only thing I heard him say was "You will get a copy of the support order in the mail in a week or so. Thank you for dialing in. Okay were going to hang up now."

...dial tone

Hello...Hello

I think back on that day and if I knew then what I know now it could have all been avoided had I knew how to deal with conflict, had better communication and made a commitment to follow through with things involving our children. You see, I needed to find harmony in my life because this was new territory, and I could not begin the healing process due to the fact that I was so caught up in my feelings about past issues and I didn't know who I really was.

This one incident changed my life as I have been a coparent for over 20 years and what I have learned from this as well as my other life experiences, conversations and research from other coparents is that there was a substantial need for a program that could help them resolve conflicts with the other parent. One common thing that I have learned is that issues surrounding the children combined with any past problems that the parents may have can be hard on everyone, and it's especially hard on parents that deal with these issues from an emotional standpoint. The problem becomes evident when both parents won't come to an agreement and nothing can be resolved. Therefore, I wanted to build a program that could help coparents work to improve themselves and that is why I created "The 32K Format"

THE FOUNDATION OF THE 32K FORMAT

This program is for those coparents that have identified that there are issues between themselves and the other parent and they would like to work on these issues. As you go through this process, the hope is that you gain the self-awareness to better understand yourself. Also, as you progress through the different modules, you will be able to see your level of growth on your journey of transformation to becoming a better person and a better parent.

Let's break it down. The 32K Format stands for:

3 = Three C's (Conflict, Communication and Commitment)
2 = Two H's (Harmony and Healing)
K = Know You

So, without further ado...LET'S GET STARTED!

The 3 C's

<u>CONFLICT</u>

Coparenting with someone who you constantly have problems with is one of the most challenging issues parents will face. It may seem impossible at the onset, but it is possible to overcome conflict in coparenting and peacefully raise your children as partners in parenting. Consider the following strategies to overcome conflict.

MODULE 1K: Your Child Always Comes First

So that there is no misunderstanding; the children's needs always comes first. One of your goals as a coparent should be to meet your children's needs and reach agreements with the other parent that work in best interest of your children before you begin focusing on your own desires. Maybe the other parent is telling you that they want to reschedule their parenting time...AGAIN. Or maybe the other parent is insisting on being the person to contact on all the school information forms. You know those questions you get asked that tend to make you think to yourself "is there something that I'm missing" or is what the other parent asking really that important?

You see sometimes you can get so caught up with what you think is important that you forget that the two of you should be thinking about the children's needs first. If you take the time to think about what you are doing by not making the situation about you and the other parent, this can help you and the other parent with keeping the focus on your children first and not your own issues.

Module 2K: Let The Past Be The Past

As coparents, you should focus on what's happening now with your children and not what happened between you and the other parent in the past.

There's a saying, "where your focus goes, your energy flows" and that is so true because if you get stuck on past conflicts or events that contributed to why you are not with the other parent anymore, it could lead you to make decisions based on your memories and not on things that are in the best interest of the children.

Side Note:
Forgiving the other parent or yourself may seem impossible, but it's not. Forgiveness is actually something you do for yourself and your children. Divorce and mediation can be difficult processes to endure. The ability to forgive will lighten the emotional burden you are carrying and make it easier to be a good parent and an effective coparent.

Make a commitment to yourself to do what you have to do to feel better. Forgiveness is for you and not for anyone else.

Forgiveness does not necessarily mean reconciliation with the person that hurt you or condoning their action. What you are after is to find peace. Forgiveness can be defined as the "peace and understanding that come from blaming that which has hurt you less, taking the life experience less personally, and changing your grievance story.

Get the right perspective on what is happening. Recognize that your primary distress is coming from the hurt feelings, thoughts, and physical upset you are suffering now, not what offended you or hurt you two minutes or ten years ago. Forgiveness helps to heal those hurt feelings.

The practice of forgiveness has been shown to reduce anger, hurt, depression, and stress and leads to greater feelings of hope, peace, compassion, and self-confidence. Practicing forgiveness leads to healthy relationships as well as physical health. It will also help couples cope through divorce proceedings and mediation.

Module 3K: Don't Let Conflict Scare You

Being afraid of conflict may cause a person to become more defensive or irritated than they normally would be in a conversation. If you sense a conversation or situation about to occur that could create conflict, there's one simple thing that you can do as a first step. It's quite simple if you think about it and that is to take a deep breath and keep calm in order to reduce any tension that could make this situation go from what could be a civil discussion to a full-on dispute.

Module 4K: Clarify, Don't Assume

We should do all that we can to avoid making assumptions. However, when facing whatever the conflict is, it may be easy to overthink the situation and make assumptions about the other parent's actions.

It can sometimes be hard not to make assumptions when having a conversation with someone, especially if it's someone whom you may not be getting along with at the moment. Part of being a good communicator means giving the other person in the conversation a chance to share their ideas so that you may contemplate them without jumping to conclusions. Do your best to let any assumptions go before communicating with the other parent. If you're not sure what the other parent is trying to tell you, ask questions that will help you get the answers you are looking for.

Module 5K: Give Yourself A Chance to Think

It can be hard to know what to say when you are confronted with a difficult situation. To help you overcome either the conflict that is coming, that conflict you are currently in or the conflict that you may be getting out of, you will want to focus on how you want to respond to the situation.

So, the next time that you are faced with a conflict between yourself and the other parent, you need to give yourself some time to really think about what it is that you want to say and how to do so in a constructive manner in order to get your point across.

Module 6K: Winning Isn't Everything

Overcoming conflict in coparenting is not going to be easy and it also isn't just about winning arguments in order to end them. It's about communicating and reaching agreements in such a way that not only upholds your children's best interests but also keeps them protected from conflict that can be harmful to them (notice that I said, "your children" and not you).

To work on this, you will need to let go of always trying to be right because, the truth is, you may not always be and does it really matter at the end of the day. Instead, make an effort to have a level of understanding. Keeping the focus on your child and their best interest, not yours, will help make this attainable.

Side Note:
No one ever said coparenting will be easy. But it's a challenge worth stepping up for. Because your kids will be affected by every decision, action and conflict you, as coparents, create.

Believe me, those same kids will hold you responsible when they grow up and ask you, "Why did you do that? What were you thinking?"

Don't they deserve better than that?

Module 7K: This Is A Business

The relationship that you have with the other parent became a business the moment that you and the other parent chose not to be together anymore. And now the business that the two of you are in is coparenting together.

One thing that you need to understand is that emotional attachments and expectations don't work in business relationships. Just like in a business, you need to try and achieve successful business communication by being up-front and direct, appointments need to be scheduled, meetings need to take place, agendas are to be provided, discussions focus on the business at hand, everyone is polite, formal courtesies are observed, and agreements are explicit, clear, and written.

Understand that you do not need to like the people you do business with but you do need to put negative feelings aside in order to conduct business. Relating in a business-like way with your coparent may feel counter-productive but it will come in handy if you catch yourself or the other parent behaving in a nonbusiness-like way.

Side Note:
Any successful business has a common goal. As a coparenting couple, your goal is to raise healthy children and every coparenting decision you make together is decided based on how this will affect our business goal: healthy thriving children. As two invested partners in this business, you both are making decisions based on this one very important common goal. Since you are both invested in this business, you would not publicly put your business down on social media or to your family members or friends. You would promote your coparenting business to everyone! Remember your business is raising healthy children! In raising healthy, thriving children, it is vital that children hear good things about each parent because each parent is a part of them. When you put down one parent, you are putting down 50% of that child, thus hurting your coparenting business and your child.

Module 8K: A Time And Place For Apologies

Placing blame is very rarely an effective way to end a conflict. But its counterpart, admitting fault, can help resolve conflicts that come from the mistakes that coparents will make. If you make a mistake, own it and apologize as soon as possible to avoid any other issues that may come up.

It is just as important to give an apology as it is to receive one. No one is perfect and we need to understand that everyone makes mistakes. So, when and if an apology comes your way, just take it at face value and do not punish the other parent for whatever mistake they are admitting to.

Side Note:
Just like there are good apologies, there also bad apologies.

If you have ever apologized in any of the following ways, it's possible that you are an ineffective apologizer:
- "I'm sorry but you also…"
    - The word "but" minimizes the apology
- Apologizing when you don't mean it

- The other person will always know if it's not genuine
- "I didn't mean to upset you…"
  The impact of something can be hurtful even if the intention was not

Module 9K: Seek Solutions, Not Retaliation

Retaliation will get you nothing and only prolongs the situation. As a result, coparents can easily get stuck doing meaningless tit-for-tats unless they break the cycle.

Instead of approaching a conflict to finger point, think of it as a situation that requires each coparent with a chance to work together to resolve the issue.

It's not going to be easy at first, but approach each conflict as an opportunity to improve your coparenting efforts, rather than another chance to play the blame-game. It will be more effective in the long run.

Module 10K: Be Open To Other Possibilities

While you are in the middle of a conflict, it's easy to get tunnel vision. You may feel that you know the best way out of the situation, and you refuse to consider other options. Whether you are consciously doing this or not, you may be coming off as unreasonable to the other parent.

For conflict resolution, however, it's important for you to resist becoming narrow-minded to other solutions that are not yours. Contrary to what you may believe, there is more than one way to resolve an issue.

Module 11K: Coparent, Don't Counter-parent

As a coparent, you are expected to somehow overcome the ugliness of you past relationships and still function as a normal parent. The reality is that this can be more difficult than it sounds and, to be honest, many parents fail at it! The difficult task is finding a way to maintain a cordial relationship, with a person you probably don't want to speak to.

The question you have to ask is: are you coparenting or counter-parenting?

You may not be friends with the other parent, agree with or even like them; but you have to push negative feelings to the side to make decisions, be present, and still be a parent to your children.

Counter-parents maintain their hate and anger for the other parent. They can't forgive, let alone forget, and every encounter is an opportunity to remind the other parent of how much they dislike them and to possibly enact some revenge for the past

Coparenting is one of the most difficult things any of us will ever do! It requires a thick skin, infinite patience, and the vision to see that even though the relationship with the other parent didn't survive, the commitment to parent is forever.

Of course, the process is easier when both parties are willing to invest in the process instead of avoiding their responsibilities or seeking conflict.

Even if the other parent engages in counter-parenting, your children deserve your best efforts to coparent. If nothing else, they should see one parent keep their word, act in their best interest, and set a good example. So, coparent or counter-parent: the choice is yours, but your children are counting on you!

Module 12K: Relieve Stress and Take Your Time

In order to approach conflict resolution with a cooperative mindset, coparents need to be able to actively practice empathy. Stress is an emotion that is commonly experienced during conflict and it isn't conducive to resolving the issue.

To counteract those strong emotions, parents should know which stress-relieving methods work for them. Practicing stress relief during conflict is not only good for your blood pressure, but it also gives you a chance to consider what approach you will take as opposed to simply reacting to whatever it is.

Goals and Journal Page

_____

_____

_____

_____

_____

_____

_____

_____

_____

_____

_____

_____

_____

_____

COMMUNICATION

People often say they do not like communicating with their coparent because they are exhausted from the chaos that it brings. No one said that it would be easy and sometimes you might want to throw your hands up and just avoid it all together. But for the benefit of your children, as long as the point of it is to be effective and constructive, you have to make an effort to have what may seem like an uncomfortable conversation.

In order to put yourself on the road to successfully resolving conflicts, communication between coparents must be healthy. The communication troubles experienced when parents were together does not magically disappear once they begin their coparenting. So it's important that coparents not only recognize their bad habits when it comes to communicating but that they also actively work to correct those tendencies.

As long as you are dedicated to creating a better life for your children, the following building blocks of effective communication: avoiding communication blocks, language, delivery, listening, and consistency are elements that can help to improve the way that you and your coparent communicate, which will also help you to build a more solid relationship as partners in parenting.

Module 13K: Avoid Communication Blocks

Many times, communication breaks down between coparents because one of the parties blocks the lines of communication. Sometimes it's done deliberately and sometimes it's subconscious. It helps to have self-awareness and recognize the common ways that communication gets blocked. They are: interrupting, giving advice, invalidating the other parent, being defensive, being critical, or having contempt.

Side Note:
Although there is no magic formula for ensuring a positive outcome after separating, these tips will lead to effective communication with your former spouse and coparenting easier to manage after your divorce. Remember, children need to know that their parents love them – not only in words, but also in the actions they take as coparents.

Module 14K: Language

Effective communication greatly relies on language and word choice. Saying the wrong thing at the wrong time can quickly take a conversation down an unintended path. Words can sometimes be misconstrued and given new meaning by the listener, so it is important to choose wisely.

Choose the right words to properly convey what you need to say. Avoid language that serves no other purpose than to hurt the other person. This would include name calling, vulgar language, and sarcasm.

Module 15K: Delivery

Just like how word choice is important, the way you deliver those words is just as relevant towards building effective communication. Your method of delivery (whether it is via telephone, e-mail, text, in-person, etc.), the tone of the message, and timing are all aspects to consider when communicating. You may only need one way to communicate successfully or some parents may be open to communicating in different ways. Just as long as the communication is accurate and effective.

Choose a method that allows you to accurately deliver your message. Depending on what you're talking about and how well you communicate with the other parent, you will need to decide which method is the best way to convey certain messages. But even when using your method of choice, tone still carries a lot of weight.

The tone of the communication isn't all based on the words you choose. Your expression speaks volumes and can change the tone of what you're trying to say and the way that the message may be intended.

Finally, timing can also have a huge impact on how a person receives a message. For example, when coparents exchange the children, that probably isn't the best time to bring up touchy subjects with the other parent. Keep more serious conversations reserved for times when you and your coparent can properly focus on the matter at hand without putting your kids in the middle of conflict.

Module 16K: Listening

The foundation for good communication lies in the ability to listen. Listening to and trying to understand the other parent is more important than you may realize.

Listening is a skill, and we tend to do it naturally with people that we are close to but it doesn't come so easily when we are trying to work with a coparent and emotions are involved. If applied effectively, it can be beneficial to everyone.

There are times to talk, and there are times to listen. It is often true that moments of listening are just as, if not more, crucial to building effective communication between coparents. When you do not properly hear what the other person has to say, how are you supposed to make an attempt to respond?

Be attentive during conversations with the other parent by listening carefully or completely reading messages you receive. Don't jump to respond. Take a moment to consider what you've heard, then formulate your response. If you don't know what to say or feel as if you're about to explode, it is okay to say that you need to talk about this later. Don't forget the conversation, though. Come back to it when you are ready to focus and give a calm, effective response.

Module 17K: Consistency

If you're trying to overcome poor communication habits that you've learned, consistently practicing effective communication techniques will be key to making real and lasting change. Set yourself up for success by always having a clear picture of why you're trying to change the way you communicate, and practice the following techniques:

- Commit to regularly checking in with your coparent about your children
- Plan for conversations ahead of time in order to give it your full attention
- Be consistent about sharing concerns you have right away. Don't let issues or bad feelings fester.
- Maintain open lines of communication so you can work together as a team, rather than unknowingly countering each other's efforts

Goals and Journal Page

COMMITMENT

Coparenting requires a commitment by both parents to become better versions of themselves to ensure that their coparenting relationship is one that is cordial, focusing specifically on addressing the needs of the children. This not an all-encompassing list but committing to doing the following will put coparents on the path to success and ensuring their children are being raised in a healthy environment!

Module 18K: Control What You Can Control

It's much easier to work together as coparents when you establish boundaries and recognize what you have control over—and what you don't—regarding your children and the other parent.

For example, you cannot control who the other parent dates or even whether they introduce that person to your children (unless it's written into your custody agreement or parenting plan). You can, however, control the example you're setting for your kids when it comes to dealing with disappointments and setbacks.

Module 19K: Agree and Stick To A Schedule

Parenting time transitions are more manageable for everyone involved when the schedule represents a solid, predetermined routine, rather than an iffy, "we'll see" type of arrangement.

Coparents that can reach a healthy level of communication know that they can count on the other parent to maintain their commitments unless something truly extraordinary requires a change in the routine.

Module 20K: Be Flexible

While routine is healthy, it's also important to be flexible with the other parent. Think of it in this way, "Do unto others as you would have them do unto you." Meaning that it's better to have a healthy approach and to be as accommodating with the other parent as you'd like them to be with you.

Even if you suspect that the same courtesy may not be returned to you. If you show the way you'd like things to be between you and the other parent can be more effective than repeatedly telling the other parent how bad things are. Instead, try flipping the negative situation to find the positive.

Module 21K: Stay Focused

When talking to the other parent, focus the conversation on the specific business related to your child and do your best to talk about one child-related issue at a time. Also, be concise, to the point and do not bring up unresolved relationship issues.

Module 22K: Seek Solutions

If there is a child-related problem, first clarify the problem. Then start offering solutions that could work for the child and for both parents. This may take some creative thinking and some compromise. Keep throwing out solutions until you find one that you can both agree on.

Goals and Journal Page

The 2 H's

HARMONY

We've always heard about trying to find the balance in life. Well, balance requires something that would make it 50/50 or if it was uneven, you'd be looking at 60/40 or 70/30. Either way it requires the other person to carry their weight. Let's be real, you have to always do your best to give 100% because you can only control what you do. That's why, when life gets in the way, as much as we may try to adjust the scales to create a balance, we often end up feeling wobbly rather than balanced, and that is why we should strive for harmony instead of balance.

Harmony is more about being in tune with the life you want to have and finding a way to bring everything into alignment. Here are a few practices that will help you create more harmony and connection with yourself and in your relationship with the other parent.

Module 23K: From Resistance and To Acceptance

When you resist what is, you unconsciously resist your ability to create harmony in your relationships. This is bound to create tension, but that tension is eliminated once you consciously move into the energy of acceptance.

When you are working with the other parent, know that you cannot control them. You have to accept the fact that they are who they are and not the version you wish them to be. Allow them to grow and transform at their own pace and continually choose to accept them exactly as they are in each moment.

Module 24K: Have Compassion

When you embody compassion, you choose to respond, instead of jumping into reactions and assumptions, and this opens up a communication flow that is free from judgement. With compassion comes grace, and you give the other parent the grace to go work through their own issues. Your compassionate understanding stems from that grace and the desire for harmony and the understanding that most people haven't been shown a very good example of this.

Even if a topic is heated or opinions are conflicting, it can still be addressed from a place of compassion. This is how you practice choosing harmony over drama.

Goals and Journal Page

HEALING

To be a good coparent, first heal yourself. If one or both parents have not done the work to move on from their past, they will bring the same hurt into the coparenting relationship. When parents are combative, even the smallest decision, like whether a child can go on a school field trip can take on a life of its own. To avoid this, view the relationship as a completed one, instead of a failed one. "Self-reflect and own your role in ending the relationship." When you are happier individually, it's easier to coparent with focus and intention.

Coparenting is about your kids and not the relationship you once had with the other parent. But often we get our emotions involved and we let our anger and past hurts get in the way of what is in the best interest of the children. Let's take a look at a few of the main issues coparents face and see if we can build a successful strategy for diffusing the problem.

Module 25K: Unresolved Anger Towards The Other Parent

Of course, you may very well have justifiable anger towards the actions, or your perceived actions, of the other parent. however, in order to grow, you must take ownership of your own unresolved anger issues. Take your anger out of the coparenting relationship and get some counseling or coaching on your own. Anger is not about your coparent. Anger that bubbles over into your parenting relationship must be addressed.

It is your responsibility to take charge of your emotional state and anger may be a factor preventing you from moving on with your life. If left unchecked, this anger will certainly prevent you from forming a future healthy relationship with the other parent.

Module 26K: Social Media Venting

It's as simple as this. Just don't do it. Unfollow, unfriend, and disconnect from each other's social media accounts. You may think that staying connected via social media will lessen your anguish over the time you lose with your kids. You may want to remain "friends" but it's not a healthy idea. It takes a lot of emotional muscle for a coparent to look at photos of their kids having a good time with the other parent and not feel any regret, sadness, or anger. So, the best advice is not to post about your relationship with the other parent on social media at all and let your coparents parenting memories be theirs alone.

Module 27K: Boundary Problems

The other parent might not be the easiest of people to get along with. They may make an unreasonable request for schedule changes at the last minute. The day-before text about a next-day change, "I'd like to take the kids to out of town this weekend, can we swap out for next weekend with you," is not okay.

- Be firm with your boundaries and flexible with your children's needs. Sure, if your kids have an opportunity to go to some place special by swapping a few weekends with you, go for it, but don't let the other parent make last-minute changes or unreasonable demands that negatively impact yours or your children's lives.
- Even if your coparent has the right intention in mind, their requests and behaviors need to keep a healthy respect for you and the children.
- When in doubt, return to the official parenting plan.
- Be flexible when you can, and negotiate unemotionally when possible.
- Hold yourself to the same high standard of courtesy when requesting

a schedule change or some other coparenting negotiation.
- Kindness is king so always try to negotiate with your coparent towards a healthy result.

Goals and Journal Page

The K

KNOW YOU

Now this may seem to go against everything that you have heard or been taught but through this process you will realize that you need to do a lot of self-reflecting and working on yourself first. Parents put their children first, and it's a tough job, but realistically you can't change the way you parent or the way you interact with the other parent without first understanding who you are, why you react the way you do and knowing that you will need to change your mindset in order to move forward and transform into a better version of the current you.

Module 28K: Don't Lose Yourself

When you become a coparent, it's easy to lose yourself. You can easily get stuck in survival mode. This means that you're doing everything to look after your children and all that you think that is needed for them but you're doing nothing for yourself. No matter how you came to be a coparent, you might feel as though you are constantly in a cycle of being needed. The thing that you might not even realize is how truly stuck you are. Maybe you are just exhausted, combined with a feeling of dissatisfaction, and you just don't feel as though you are making any progress in your personal life.

As a coparent, you may feel like you're always juggling things and it might seem ridiculous to even have the notion that you will have time to do anything for yourself. Just know that making time for yourself is very important, perhaps even more so than you think.

Module 29K: Don't Lose Your Confidence

Losing confidence in yourself can be like getting stuck in quicksand because it disables you. It doesn't take you anywhere because it makes you afraid of life and of living freely. This type of negative thinking has a similar outcome since it holds you back and seemingly won't allow you to move forward.

If you begin thinking that your situation is hopeless or won't change, then it could have a negative effect on your outlook and you won't go after things if you don't believe you can have them. This is a vicious cycle and you can get stuck in it if you don't recognize it in time.

No matter what obstacles lie in your path, tell yourself that you CAN do it, you WILL do it, you are WORTHY of it. Life might be hard, but if you push yourself forward, and start doing all those things that you want to do and somewhere deep inside believe you can do it, then you can open the door to rediscovering the real YOU.

Module 30K: Be Aware of Your Trigger Points

Triggers are those things that when they happen, you have an involuntary negative response. Depending on the way you were raised as a child and who you are now as a person, the trigger may make you feel angry, shut down, get upset, feel out of control or feel like you want to take your aggression out on someone else.

Now that you know what a trigger point is, it's important that you try to identify what your trigger points are so that you can take control of what it is that you have been letting control you.

Figuring out what your trigger points are and identifying your emotional triggers is so vital. Until you bring to your awareness what provokes extreme responses from you, you'll constantly be manipulated by your emotions. And thus, your relationship with the other parent could be strained, ruined, turbulent or sabotaged. Your life, in general, will seemingly be much more painful.

It really is worth putting in the effort to explore your emotional triggers. The more aware you are, the less you will be ruled by the unconscious forces within you. The most difficult part to exploring your triggers is actually committing and being open to the process.

So here is a way to find your trigger points:

What Thoughts Are Running Through Your Head

Look for extreme thoughts with polarized viewpoints (i.e. someone or something is good/bad, right/wrong, etc.). You don't have to do anything else but be aware of these thoughts without reacting to them. Let them play out in your mind. What story is your mind creating about the other person or situation? Making a list of these thoughts will definitely enhance your self-awareness.

Who Or What Triggered The Emotion?

Once you have become aware of your physical reactions (or in conjunction with this practice), notice who or what has triggered the extreme physical and emotional responses within you. Sometimes you will discover a single object, word, smell or another sense impression that triggers you. Other times, you will notice that you are triggered by a certain belief, viewpoint, or overall situation. Not only that, but you may have multiple triggers, so be vigilant and open to perceiving a whole spectrum of things that set you off. As always, it's important that your record these triggers in some kind of journal (whether a printed one or a digital one). Writing down these triggers will help to sear them into your mind so that you remain self-aware in the future.

What To Do Once You've Been Triggered
So let's just say that you've done everything you know of to prevent yourself from being triggered but you still find yourself about to lose it... so what can you do next?

Here are some practices to consider:
- **Breathe**
  So long as you're alive, you're breathing and therefore let's use it as an excellent way to relax. Try focusing on slowly breathing in your nose and out your mouth for a few minutes. If your attention goes

back to the triggering person or situation, pull your attention back to your breathing.

- **Break Away**
Remove yourself from the situation. Step away for five minutes and cool down. If you are speaking with someone, excuse yourself temporarily and say that you need to go to the bathroom or someplace else. Return when you are calm.

- **Find The Humor**
Now don't get me wrong, when I say humor, I'm not just talking about laughing because that this might not always be possible. I mean looking at the situation as a whole from a bird's eye perspective and finding the comicality of it.

Knowing your own personal trigger points can be helpful in effectively interacting with the other parent and by recognizing them before and while they happen. Having that sense of awareness will give you better control over your response and it will help you to become less reactive

Module 31K: Your Personality Is The Key

When you are at the stage in your life where you are open to having an idea of who you truly are, you will begin to have a better understanding of all the different reactions and perceptions that other people might have to the same situations. We all have a different way of seeing and interacting with the world.

One statement rings true when it comes to trying to understand why people act the way that they do and that is "common sense ain't that common" meaning that you can't expect people to act the same way that you do in certain situations because we are all wired differently and have different upbringings. You see, people often mistakenly believe that most other people share the same views, opinions, attitudes, and traits that they do.

Understanding some of your personality traits as well as those of the people you interact with is helpful in building coparenting relationships. By better knowing your own personality traits, it will give you better insight as to how best to respond and communicate with the other parent.

Once you have an idea of what your specific personality type is, you can improve your interactions and communication with the other parent by following a few examples of Do's and Don'ts to transform yourself into a better parent and communicator:

Do:
- Be consistent in your approaches
- Be responsive
- Be respectful and acknowledge

Don't:
- Act on anger
- Presume or jump to conclusions
- Try to control everything

Module 32K: Self-Care

Self-care is an important part of daily life, however during times of conflict with the coparent, the need for self-care is imperative. It refers to the activities and practices that you deliberately choose to engage in on a regular basis to maintain and enhance your health and wellbeing. It helps to prevent stress and anxiety as well as making you more effective when you face challenges.

Self-care is often the first thing that gets sacrificed when life is busy and stressful, and people often think that taking time for themselves can wait. But looking after your own wellbeing will help you get through those challenging times and will help you to better care for others.

So, keep it simple, during times of conflict, implementing a self-care plan can help you focus, make decisions and stay healthy

Goals and Journal Page

THANK YOU!

Thank you for reading *The 32K Format: The Coparents Transformation Guide To Becoming A Better Person And Parent.* I hope that you keep the momentum going because this isn't the end of your journey but rather the beginning of creating a productive future for yourself and your children.

www.ingramcontent.com/pod-product-compliance
Lightning Source LLC
Chambersburg PA
CBHW071412290426
44108CB00014B/1785